Copyright © 2020 by Philips Coleman Ph.d

All rights reserved. No part of this publication may be reproduced, distributed, or transmitted in any form or by any means, including photocopying, recording, or other electronic or mechanical methods, without the prior written permission of the publisher, except in the case of brief quotation embodied in critical reviews and certian other noncommercial uses permitted by copyright law.

Table of Contents

Introduction ... 3
What is Facebook Marketing? ... 6
Why is Facebook good for marketing? ... 9
Formats of Facebook Marketing ... 13
What do you need to succeed in Facebook marketing? ... 19
Why aren't people seeing my posts? ... 25
    Why are Facebook algorithms such a big deal? ... 25
    The components of Facebook algorithms ... 28
How to Create an Effective Facebook Marketing Strategy ... 32
How can I get more views on my business' Facebook posts? ... 52
Benefits of Facebook Marketing ... 59
Advantages of Facebook marketing ... 65
Disadvantages of Facebook marketing ... 68
How to Get Started with Facebook Marketing for your online store? ... 71
Conclusion ... 80

Introduction

Facebook isn't new, and neither is the idea that every business needs a Facebook presence. However, a lot has changed since Facebook first entered the marketing scene. Today, the world's largest social network can do things many of us would never have dreamed of 10 years ago: host 360-degree videos, sell products via a chatbot, or even serve as a top news source for two-thirds of the adult population. Facebook has 1.56 billion daily active users . Let's put that in perspective. That's nearly

5X the population of the United States, 20% of the world population and still climbing. So imagine the social influence achievable through Facebook in terms of your peer effects, ecommerce business, referrals, customer relationships, reputation, brand awareness, and much more (let alone, in combination with other social media platforms you market through). It's not only the sheer number of people but the amount of our attention Facebook owns. Globally, the average user spends almost an hour per day on Facebook. Considering the average person sleeps eight hours a day, that means about 7% of our waking hours is spent with our eyes glued to the social network.

What is Facebook Marketing?

There are actually two sides to Facebook marketing. One major part falls under the umbrella of traditional social media marketing (SMM) and the other is akin to a highly-targeted ad campaign. Depending on your specific business model, one or both sides to Facebook marketing may suit your needs. If you're like most successful online store owners, your overall marketing strategy will include a combination of social media marketing and targeted ads on Facebook.

A note about neigh-sayers: Facebook marketing has changed quite a bit in the past few years. So much so that some misguided marketers may even tell you that it has become irrelevant and that you shouldn't waste your time. Unfortunately, that is some very bad advice. Why do people feel this way? Probably because they have tried marketing on Facebook and failed. Don't let their failure predict your outcome. It has nothing to do with you. There is no one-size-fits-all approach. You must be willing to roll up your sleeves to do the market research, create a strategy a put it to work for you.

Why is Facebook good for marketing?

Digital marketing offers a variety of channels for building communication with the audience: social media, emails, messengers, search engines, SMS, web push notifications, etc. Let's get a closer look at the reasons why you should consider Facebook as a platform for growing your business:

Has global coverage. Over 1,5 billion users visit Facebook daily. About 2,3 billion — every month.

More than 7 million active companies create ads for this massive audience.

Offers highly targeted paid ads. With Facebook Ads, you can tailor your promotions to a specific audience based on gender, age, location, job, interests — any demographical or behavioral data, which users willingly share with Facebook.

Makes organic reach possible. If you don't have resources to utilize Facebook Ads, build relationships organically by sharing materials that bring value to people on your Facebook page. Your posts will show up in the newsfeed, though the high level of competition will make it harder to build an audience naturally.

Allows integrations with other marketing channels. Facebook marketing is not a single isolated system. You can combine it with other marketing channels, like email marketing, mobile marketing, search engine marketing, and Facebook Messenger ads, to develop a promotion mix that will increase your brand outreach.

Formats of Facebook Marketing

Facebook is not only a social media leader but also a fast-growing company due to half a million new accounts created per day. As time goes by, Facebook developers come up with new formats of ads to meet modern requirements of Facebook Ads funnel building, optimizing the time-proven ads. Here's a list of Facebook marketing formats:

Video ad

It is an excellent way to demonstrate the features of your product in action. Facebook allows using different types of video to meet specific goals: short videos and GIFs to quickly capture attention on a go, or In-Stream videos for a longer TV-like watching.

Image ads

In case your budget is too tight to make a video, image ad is a good idea for creating a high-quality ad fast and easy. This format will help you raise brand awareness and drive people to your website.

Carousel ads

This format allows showcasing up to ten images or videos inside a single advertisement — each with a link to a specific product page. It provides a vast field for creativity and interactivity since you can feature one product in detail, or a few different products, or tell a story, separated by those carousel cards.

Collection ad

It is like a small catalog of your products right in a post on the Facebook feed. A Collection ad consists of one original video or image and four smaller pictures below in the form of a grid.

Slideshow ads

It is a video-like format that displays well even if the speed of the internet connection is low. You can create such an ad using a variety of stock images, some handy tools for video editing, and even music.

Lead generation ads

This format was developed to assist in generating leads,

especially regarding mobile users. When a user taps on the image in such an advertisement, a subscription form shows up right in the ad, making a few taps enough to opt-in to your newsletters.

What do you need to succeed in Facebook marketing?

With so many active users, Facebook marketing has what seems to be unlimited potential, but there are some things you should know before you get started.

Knowledge – Facebook is a social platform, which makes it stand out from other ad platforms. This means that you have to take care to avoid overly pitchy text and behavior. Knowing how to talk to your customers when they are on social media is one of the most valuable tools you can have in your arsenal.

Staff – As an entrepreneur, you probably wear many hats. This can work to your advantage or be your biggest downfall. In the case of Facebook marketing, it can go either way. You or someone with a great deal of knowledge about your brand should be in charge of the content that you produce, including any and all comments and replies. This will ensure that your marketing efforts truly reflect your brand. Someone else can handle the other stuff that needs to be done. For example, you may hire someone to monitor Facebook groups and hashtags that are relevant to your business or evaluate and report on ad performance.

Money – A monetary investment may be made on Facebook ads, which can be highly-targeted to your desired demographic, but the investment is small compared to the quality of consumer you will reach. Because you can target an audience by things like geographic location, marital status and interests, you are likely to reach more of your potential customers with every ad.

Time – The social element of Facebook marketing is a labor of love, but it is one that can only bring you closer to your customers, resulting in a better understanding of who they are and how to reach them. It is time intensive. And we all know that time is money. Especially when we're talking about your time.

Software – There are many tools designed to help increase your engagement and overall understanding of your Facebook audience and marketing. Some of my favorite tools also include post scheduling. If you're interested in advanced planning and analytics (as you should be), check out Buffer and Hootsuite, And don't forget about Facebook's own tools: Insight, e timPages to Watch and its Pages app. If you want to run contests, tools like ShortStack can very valuable.

Creativity – About 300 million photos are uploaded to Facebook every day. It isn't Instagram (link to Instagram post) or Pinterest (link to Pinterest post), but it is very visual nonetheless. Your posts should be somewhat varied between text, links and images, but don't be afraid to go heavy on the image posts. Images are also crucial in Facebook advertising. They should represent your brand and grab a user's attention within seconds (no small task).

Why aren't people seeing my posts?

Why are Facebook algorithms such a big deal?

Nobody's 100% sure how Facebook's algorithms work — they're a very, very closely guarded secret. But that doesn't mean Facebook hasn't given us lots of clues. Basically, whenever you "like" or share a "reaction" to a post or a page, Facebook takes that into account whenever it loads up for you. Every "like" and "reaction" tells Facebook's algorithm what you like or don't like, and its algorithm springs into action.There are likely thousands of what are called "weight factors" to consider, tailored for each one of Facebook's 2 billion members. (More on what these terms mean in a sec.)Every time you open Facebook, the algorithms take into consideration everything that you share, what your friends and people/pages you follow share, how you react to those things, how your friends react, and so on – and it serves up a bespoke News Feed, just for you, and for each of your fans. In short: The better you understand how Facebook decides who sees your updates, the more strategic you can be.

The components of Facebook algorithms

"Affinity," "weight," and "time decay" are aspects of an algorithm that work together to determine which users will see your post on their timeline.

Let's break it down a bit more:

Affinity

A Facebook user's "affinity" with your page depends on how often and in what ways they interact with you. The more a user likes, shares, clicks, and comments on your page posts, the more of you and your business they'll see in their Facebook timeline.

Weight

Weight refers to the value of a post based on what kind of post it is. For example, posts that include photos, links, and videos may have a higher weight than those that don't. And if that weren't hard enough to keep track of alone, weight increases the more users interact with a post. So, a post without a photo that got a bunch of likes or comments might be weighted more heavily than a photo post with no engagement at all.

Time Decay

Facebook posts lose value with age. The longer your post has been active, the less frequently it'll show up in the Feeds of people who've liked your business' page. (That's why resharing content can be such a powerful tool in your Facebook marketing toolbox!)

How to Create an Effective Facebook Marketing Strategy

It doesn't matter which channel you use, you need to develop a strategy. This will help you clearly establish your goals, choose the best techniques to reach them, define your target audience, measure the effectiveness of your campaigns, and improve. Below, we outline a plan that is universal for any business wanting to develop a Facebook marketing strategy.

Set your goals

It all starts with goal establishment. Regardless of your business type, the general goals are the same for each company. Facebook offers opportunities to reach the following goals:

generating leads;

nurturing and qualifying your leads;

driving traffic to a website;

increasing conversions and sales;

improving customer support;

raising brand awareness;

boosting customer engagement;

recruitment.

Your goal predetermines the techniques, posts, and ad formats that you will use to achieve it. You can break down your goal into small intermediate objectives. Thus, achieving each of them will make you closer to reaching your big goal. Lastly, create a list of KPIs, that you will use to measure the effectiveness of each technique.

Define your target audience

Analyzing your target audience is a high priority task since it will predetermine the techniques, ad formats, and your tone of voice. Firstly, we recommend that you answer the following questions:

Is your product for men or women?

How old are your customers?

What are their most common jobs?

What problem do they have in common?

Why should they use your product?

What outcomes do they want to achieve with it?

To collect and store all of the data about your target audience, and make the entire process more effective, create a customer profile. It should include their location, age, gender, job position, and income level information. Read our blog post to find out how to create a customer profile. Another source of information about your audience is Facebook Audience Insights. With this tool, you'll get information about people connected to your page, people from your custom audience, and people on Facebook. You can get to know what your existing audience likes, where your customers live and the language they speak, monitor their past purchasing activities, devices they use, etc.

Choose content formats and schedule posts

Now that you've defined your audience and established your goals, it's time to think over a content strategy that will help you achieve them. A content marketing strategy means that you should create a step-by-step plan which includes types and formats of content that you will produce. Remember that the more content you create, the higher your conversions will be. Using a diversity of formats, consistent publishing, and communicating with customers will skyrocket your user engagement level.

You should also take into account using the correct content mix. Promotional content itself won't help you build trusting relationships with your audience. Besides, Facebook can penalize overly-pushy marketers for their salesy promotions. So, mix educational, informative, entertaining, and promotional content. If you manage to provide high-quality and relevant content, customers will be happy to learn more about your product. To produce engaging content, you'll probably need a content maker. This is a person responsible for creativity. This specialist knows which content formats will help you best achieve your goals. Utilize images, text posts, videos, stories, and links in your strategy. When using images, keep in mind that they should be professional and high resolution. Stay away from using stock images. Videos tend to attract and engage users in the most. Take into account that a majority of users watch videos with the sound turned off, so make sure it conveys your idea even without audio. Using text, stick to 3 sentences. Your task is to use them to your advantage: to attract, provide value, and drive action. When adding a link to your website, pay special attention to the image. The last important issue is the consistency and frequency of publishing posts. We recommend that you produce 5 posts a week. This way, you don't bombard customers with your publications and will manage to craft high-quality content without brutal deadlines. For this purpose, use a content calendar. With its help, you'll have a clear picture of your content marketing strategy. Take care of all the marketing channels that you use, align each goal with a content format, and distribute them across all the channels.

So, to create an effective content marketing calendar, include the following information:

all the channels you use;

the types of content you use;

the date and time of publishing;

the topic of your post;

URL;

the image link;

the status of the post.

Luckily, Facebook provides an opportunity to schedule posts and set up auto-publishing. So, there's no need to worry about any human mistakes.

Boost your post with Facebook Ads

Facebook is an excellent advertising platform. It allows brands to reach wide audiences, provides a variety of targeting options, tools for successful outreach, and relatively cheap pricing. It is based on a bidding strategy. You choose the timing, ad placement, and target audience.

Make use of Facebook tools

Facebook provides much more value than you may expect. There's plenty of useful tools that can make your work with this channel more effective and lucrative. Check out a list of several of the tools below.

Facebook Messenger

It is an app created to stay close with your customers via text messages, video, and voice communications. With this app, you can keep your audience engaged, provide them with personalized experiences, and deliver support.SendPulse's chatbot builder allows you to create a chatbot for Facebook Messenger. It will help you deliver personalized messages to your clients, bulk messages, and auto-reply flows.

A flow imitates live conversation with a client. Delegate your routine tasks such as handling orders and bookings, answering FAQs, and providing important information, to a chatbot. You can develop a flow based on the buttons your customers click. Make use of text, images, product cards, galleries, files, lists, and other formats. The message will be sent after a user types the keyword you used when creating a bot, for example, "price," "delivery," "purchase," "refund," etc.

Measure your effectiveness

Your strategy won't work on its own. Its efficiency primarily depends on how well your audience interacts with your brand. Monitoring their engagement will help you have a clear picture of the techniques that work best for you, and those which scare away your followers.Luckily, you don't need any third-party services to track your effectiveness since Facebook offers its own tool called Insights. You'll get to know which formats work best and if your content mix was created correctly. You can check out page views, post engagement, story reach, actions on page, analyze your followers, and much more valuable data.If you want to track conversions outside Facebook, for example, bookings and purchases, make use of Google Analytics, UTM parameters, Hootsuite Insights, etc.

How to be strategic with your content when faced with an algorithm

Facebook serves up not only the content you like best, but what its algorithms think you will like. That goes for your fans, too. While the basic components of the algorithms remain the same, the algorithms themselves will change and readjust over time. That's a big reason why businesses don't feel like Facebook is a reliable way to drive organic traffic! But there is one thing that's been consistent for years: Facebook has always loved "high quality" content. (And they're totally cool with you resharing high quality content, any ol' time!)Understanding your fans and what content they like — and what content they interact with most — and then serving up that content is the genesis of the "high quality" content bar.

So it's incredibly important to become familiar with your Page Insights, and ask yourself these important questions before you post:

Are there trends in when your status updates get the most engagement or reach?

Do certain types of updates, or updates about certain subjects, perform better than others?

Is what you're posting affecting how many people see what you're sharing, both now and in the future?

Would people want to share your update with their friends or recommend it to others?

How can I get more views on my business' Facebook posts?

Experimenting with promoted posts can have big benefits, but most Page posts in a person's Feed are organic. (Curated by Facebook's algorithms, natch – not organic from Whole Foods!)In fact, the more Pages a person likes overall, the likelier it is that the Page posts they see are organic ones.So before you shell out cash for ads or spend money to promote your posts, here are some things you can do to optimize the way you use your Facebook Page to get more eyeballs on your content for free.

Share irresistible content with your fans

Easier said than done, of course, but people can tell when you've put thought into a post and when you haven't. Posts with engaging and relevant content hold more "weight," so share stuff that grabs attention and triggers people to share and comment.

Add images to every. single. post.

Choosing an eye-catching featured image to go with your update can have a huge impact on shareability.

Encourage fans to interact with your posts!

Because your "affinity" depends on creating a relationship with fans, encouraging them to like, comment, and share your posts increases the odds that they'll do just that! The more likes you have, the more chances you have to increase "affinity" with each individual user.

Respond to Facebook Messenger inquiries faster

You may notice that your favorite business Pages show visitors how quickly the company responds to inquiries via Messenger. It turns out that responding to Facebook messages in a timely manner can increase your affinity with users – plus it's just a nice thing to do!

Post questions to get fans talking!

Questions can be related to your general industry or to popular topics. An example of an industry-focused question might be, "If you could only ask a life coach one question for free, what would it be?" or "What's an app most people haven't heard of that you love?" These questions spark creativity and personal opinions, which usually help get conversations started.

Add a call to action to your posts

Need to light a (virtual) fire under your audience? A simple prompt at the end of a post can be the spark you need! Don't hesitate to tell your fans to like, share, and comment on your posts.

Most of all post and post often!

There's no way of keeping your posts from dying off, but by posting several times a day you stay in your fans' Feeds without having to worry too much about that pesky "time decay" eating up all your good Facebook karma.

Benefits of Facebook Marketing

In this section, we'll dive deeper into the advantages of using Facebook in your marketing strategy. You'll get to know which goals you can achieve with this platform apart from reaching wide audiences.

Precise targeting. You already know that Facebook allows users to deeply segment their audience but let's take a closer look at the options available. Within demographic targeting, you can select an audience with a particular income, education level, life events, relationship status, or job. You can look for customers, taking into account their interests, such as their preferred entertainment, sports, hobbies, and shopping habits. Also, you can reach clients based on purchase behaviors, intent, device usage, etc.

Increased website traffic. With this platform, you can drive your audience directly to your website. Moreover, these people will be

higher quality leads than users who land on your site organically because they already know your company. Hence, you have more credibility in their minds.
Encourage your followers to visit your site to find out more about your products. Besides, when linking to a site, Facebook generates a full-size image if your site page has one. So, it will attract many users' attention and help you boost website traffic.

Variety of ad formats. Facebook provides businesses with excellent opportunities that allow them to showcase their products from the best angles. Ads on this platform include both text and visual formats. You can boost your post by turning it into an ad, produce stories to show your behind-the-scenes, make a slideshow of your new collection, use carousel ads to demonstrate up to 10 products linking to the corresponding pages, etc.

Customer support. A lot of people prefer to connect with a brand via social media. Phone calls have become a thing of the past. Create a chatbot for Facebook Messenger to communicate with users based on their popular queries — keywords. They can include "price," "delivery," "payment options," "purchase," "book," etc. You only need to develop a scenario based on users' FAQs and write the answers. Your chatbot will imitate the real conversation. As a result, your support team will have time for more complicated issues and you can automate routine tasks.

Positive impact on SEO. Some marketers claim that social media influences search rankings. It's believed that robots take into account your data in the About section while ranking. Moreover, your social media engagement contributes a lot. Shares, likes, and comments tell Google that people are interested in your brand and engage with it. Although there is no exact proof, it isn't superfluous either.

Advantages of Facebook marketing

Massive reach – About 890 million users login to Facebook every day.

Sense of community – If you put in the time and effort, you will be rewarded with a Facebook page that acts as a community of brand advocates. It doesn't get better than this.

Advertising is easy – Instead of targeting keywords, you can target people. This works best when you know your target demographic well. And Facebook makes it easy to turn existing posts and content into ads, so you don't need to do double work.

Connect with influencers – By sharing content and tagging other brands and industry influencers, you can make connections here as easily (if not easier) than you can on Twitter.

Captive audience – Although users are there to interact with friends and family and not to purchase a product or service, you do have at least some of their attention. The average Facebook user spends about 20 minutes a day on this social networking site.

Disadvantages of Facebook marketing

Algorithm changes – Facebook is a social network built on a strong foundation of display advertising. Translation: They make A LOT of money on ads. It is no secret that this is the company's main focus. And in recent years, Facebook has taken some focus away from brand pages that do not pay to advertise. They aren't singling anyone out, of course, but their algorithm changes always seem to favor paid content. This is why a mix of paid advertising and standard social media marketing works best.

Users aren't "primed to buy" – When you run a Google Adwords campaign, you are paying to reach users when they are most likely to be ready to buy. On Facebook, people are ready to interact and be social. This just means you have to work harder to get their attention.

About 83 million fake profiles exist – Nothing is perfect, right? It is still true that 1.39 billion people use Facebook monthly, but there are also a lot of fake accounts. Some may be inactive and others may be used for less-than-ethical purposes. Don't let this dissuade you. Your audience is still out there (Facebook is working hard at eliminating those fake profiles).

How to Get Started with Facebook Marketing for your online store?

Before you jump on the Facebook marketing for ecommerce bandwagon, spend some time reviewing the network itself and the communities that are most like your brand. Then, you may start to build your strategy. Once you have your strategy ironed out, you may begin posting, but not a moment sooner!

Create a Facebook marketing strategy

Many online retailers have trouble tracking ROI on their social campaigns because they do not set proper goals. Before you even create your first post, you should know what success looks like. Only then can you create the strategy that will make it happen.

Goals – In a broad sense, what are you looking to accomplish on Facebook? Are you looking to capture email addresses? Promote brand awareness? Increase sales? Your answer may be a combination of these things, and that's okay. Just be sure to put them in order, so you can clearly define objectives in the next step.

Objectives – Now that you have your goals in order of importance, it is time to drill down to the nitty gritty. If you are looking to capture email addresses, do you have a plan for making it happen? What does success look like? Is it five emails or five thousand? How much time and effort do you expect to spend to get these emails? Be optimistic yet reasonable with your objectives.

Define Audience – Take advantage of Facebook's advanced targeting tools to clearly define your audience before you place an ad. And much like with any other advertising platform, testing is always recommended. Create an ad that goes to your core audience, your tried and true, but it's okay to test different markets and interests too. You may be pleasantly surprised.

Type of Content – To get the most out of your efforts, use all of the tools at your disposal. People like variety and they like to be entertained. Images, videos, status updates and giveaways can all help you achieve your objectives. By the way, contests are a great way to collect email addresses. Just be sure your prize is something relevant to your brand, or you may end up with email addresses that are useless to you.

Facebook Ads

If you are truly invested in Facebook marketing, your strategy will probably include Facebook ads. Ads can be used to increase likes on your Facebook page and boost visibility on your Facebook posts. But ads can also be used to drive traffic directly to your website. The ad you design should help you achieve your objectives.

Post Frequency

How often to post on Facebook is a very common question, and it is one that can vary based on the brand. I often recommend starting with one post each day and slowly introducing an additional post during peak times, such as on the weekends. Facebook's algorithm seems to favor brands that are consistent, but posting too much can dilute your message and annoy your community. This is why one post daily works well for most brands. If you happen to have something amazing or time-sensitive to say after a post has been sent, though, don't hold back. As you begin posting, keep an eye on post performance. This will tell you whether you are posting at the right times and what type of content is performing best for you. I've already mentioned Buffer and Hootsuite above, but some other tools that can help with post creation, especially on the creative end, are Pagemodo, Canva and Picmonkey.

Watch competitors

Don't get too hung up on what your competitors are doing, but you should definitely keep an eye on their pages. Use Facebook's Pages to Follow feature to help. Also, follow them and any active followers that you can. And for even more creative ideas, choose your favorite Facebook accounts from the top 500 retailers and follow them too.

Conclusion

If anyone has ever tried to talk you out of Facebook marketing, that should give you some indication that it is not easy for every brand. This does not mean that it is not worthwhile. With the right tools and know how, you can turn your Facebook page into a source of revenue for your brand. Just don't think you can set it and forget it!

www.ingramcontent.com/pod-product-compliance
Lightning Source LLC
Chambersburg PA
CBHW050252220526
45465CB00002B/646